RACCOONS

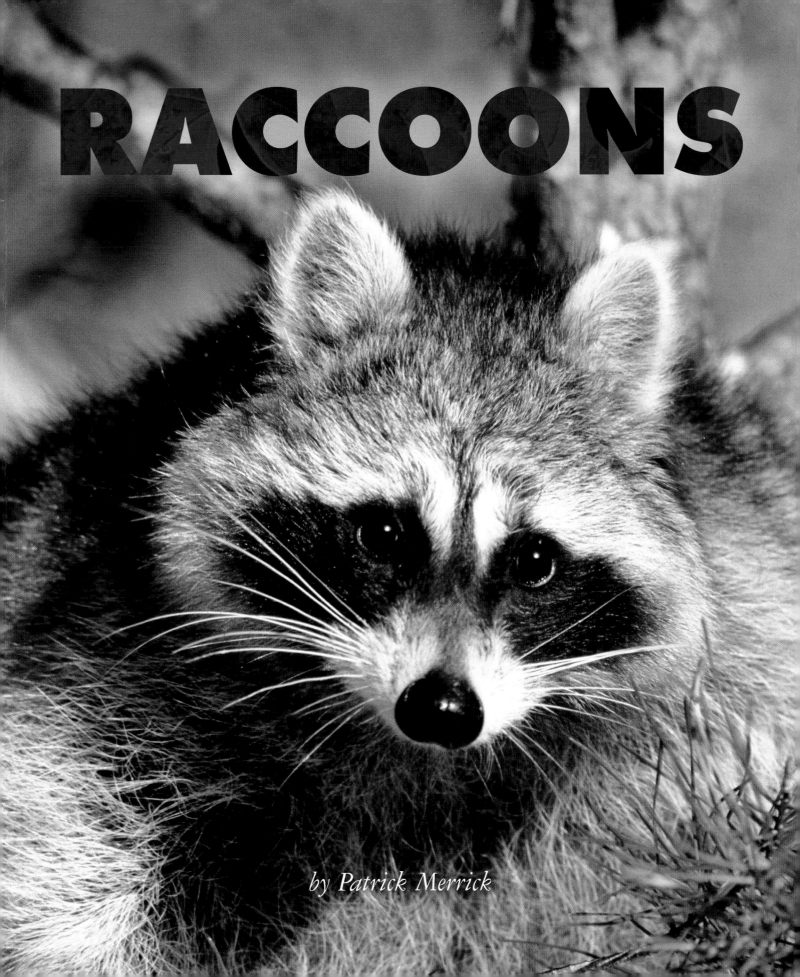

by Patrick Merrick

Content Adviser:
The Zoological Society
of San Diego

Published in the United States of America by The Child's World®
PO Box 326 • Chanhassen, MN 55317-0326
800-599-READ • www.childsworld.com

PHOTO CREDITS
© Charles Krebs/Corbis: cover, 1
© Daniel J. Cox/Getty Images: 28
© Daniel J. Cox/www.naturalexposures.com: 10, 21
© David R. Frazier Photolibrary, Inc./Alamy: 15
© Gerry Ellis/Minden Pictures: 8–9
© Joe McDonald/Corbis: 7, 16, 18–19
© John T. Fowler/Alamy: 27
© Richard A. Cooke/Corbis: 5
© Rob & Ann Simpson/Visuals Unlimited: 12–13
© Tom Brakefield/Corbis: 22–23
© Tom Tietz/Getty Images: 24

ACKNOWLEDGMENTS
The Child's World®: Mary Berendes, Publishing Director;
Katherine Stevenson, Editor

The Design Lab: Kathleen Petelinsek, Design and Page Production

LIBRARY OF CONGRESS CATALOGING-IN-PUBLICATION DATA
Merrick, Patrick.
  Raccoons / by Patrick Merrick.
     p. cm. — (New naturebooks)
  Includes bibliographical references and index.
  ISBN 1-59296-647-0 (library bound : alk. paper)
  1. Raccoons—Juvenile literature. I. Title. II. Series.
  QL737.C26M48 2006
  599.76'32—dc22   2006001375

Table of Contents

On the cover: This raccoon sitting in a pine tree was very curious about the photographer.

Meet the Raccoon!

In eastern North America, Native Americans who spoke Algonquian languages called the raccoon *arakun*—"one who scratches with his hands." Our name for the raccoon comes from that word.

It's a quiet summer evening, and you're getting ready for bed. Suddenly, you hear a loud crash outside! You look out your window and see that someone—or something—has tipped over your trash cans. Garbage is lying everywhere. In the morning, you go outside to see what happened. All you see are tracks in the dirt that look little handprints. What type of creature did this? It was one of our cutest and smartest animals—the raccoon!

These raccoon tracks were left near the Yampa River in Colorado. You can see how a raccoon's paws look a little like human hands.

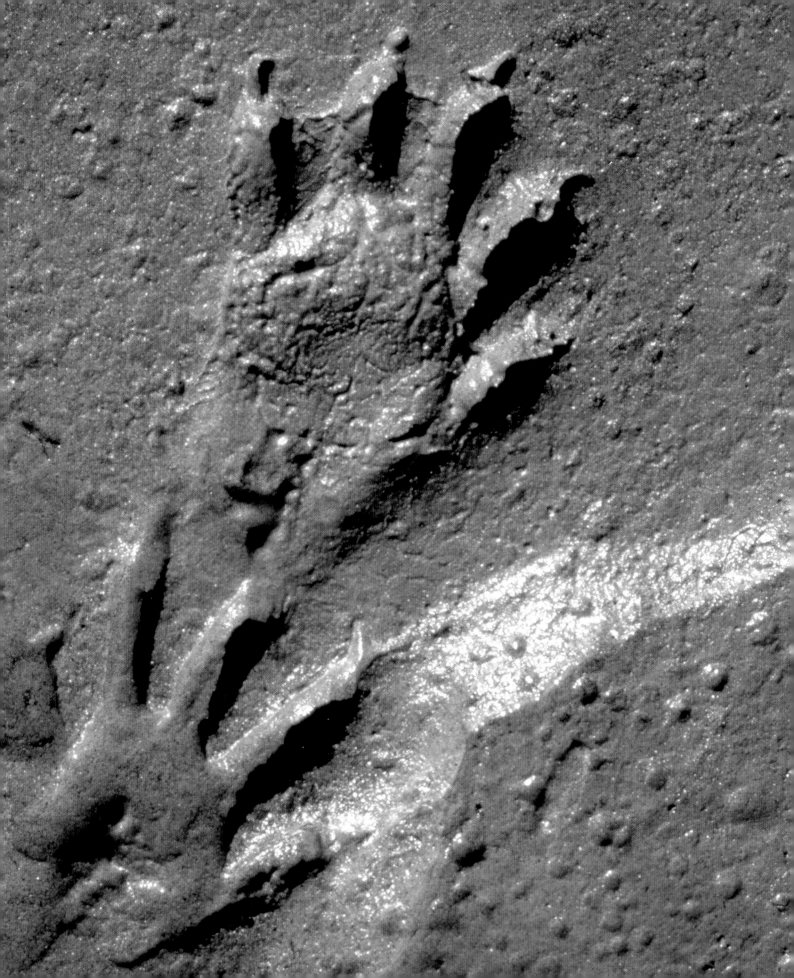

What Do Raccoons Look Like?

Adult raccoons are usually 24 to 40 inches (61 to 102 cm) long and weigh about 15 pounds (7 kg). The heaviest raccoon ever recorded weighed 62 pounds (28 kg)!

Red pandas, coatis, and kinkajous are all related to raccoons.

Raccoons have small, fat bodies covered with thick, brownish gray fur. Their noses are pointed, and their ears stick straight up. They have bushy tails with four to seven dark rings. The thing people remember best about raccoons is their black "mask." The mask is really just dark fur near the raccoon's eyes.

Raccoons belong to a group of animals called **mammals**. Mammals are covered with hair, and their bodies are warm. Mammal mothers also feed their babies milk from their bodies.

This adult raccoon climbed to the top of an old tree stump to get a better look at the photographer.

Where Do Raccoons Live?

Raccoons from North America were taken to parts of Europe and Asia and now live there in the wild.

The only environments in North America where raccoons don't live are high up in the mountains, in deserts, and in very cold regions of the far north.

Raccoons live in North, Central, and South America. There are six different kinds, or **species**, of raccoons. Only one of those species lives in North America.

Many animals can live in only one kind of place, or **environment**. Raccoons, however, can live in many different environments. The raccoons of North America prefer living in wooded areas alongside streams or lakes. They also live around swamps, in farmland, in people's backyards, and even in cities. In fact, there are lots of raccoons living in New York City, the largest city in the United States!

8

This raccoon lives in one of Washington's thick, green forests. Here it is able to find plenty of food and lots of places to hide.

Raccoons can get into lots of places where you would never expect them. They are excellent climbers and often climb high up in trees. In fact, they are one the few animals that can climb down trees headfirst! How do they do that? By turning their back feet all the way around, so that the feet point backwards and their claws can hold on. Raccoons can also drop from a great height—as much as 35 or 40 feet (11 or 12 m)—without hurting themselves.

Raccoons often make their dens inside hollow trees or logs. They also live in caves or holes in rocks, or sometimes in underground burrows. If there are no such places handy, raccoons will live in haystacks, sheds, or even attics or chimneys in people's homes. Usually, they live somewhere near water. Most raccoons stay in one den for a while, then move to a different one.

Unlike other animals, raccoons don't dig or make their own dens— they find them. Raccoon dens are either left over from other animals or in natural openings such as hollow trees or logs.

Raccoons have been seen resting in squirrels' nests or large birds' nests high up in trees.

Some raccoons use several dens at one time.

These two young raccoons are sitting high up in an aspen tree. They climbed up easily, and they'll have no trouble climbing back down again—once the photographer leaves!

11

When the first winter snow comes, a raccoon lies down in its den and goes to sleep for several days at a time. It spends most of the winter inside, coming out to eat only when it is very hungry or during warmer weather. If the winter is long and cold, the raccoon won't eat at all. It might lose up to half its body weight before spring comes again.

In colder areas, raccoons eat lots of food during the fall. They build up a thick layer of fat that helps them live through the winter.

This raccoon has made its den in the bottom of a hollow tree stump. It was in such a deep sleep, the raccoon didn't even hear the photographer.

What Do Raccoons Eat?

Raccoons are about as smart as dogs and cats. They remember places with good food and shelter.

If you go looking for raccoons during the day, all you usually find are their tracks. If you want to see a raccoon, the best time to look is at night. That's because raccoons are mostly **nocturnal**. Nocturnal animals rest during the day and are active after dark. At night, raccoons hunt for food. They can see extremely well at night, and they also have excellent hearing.

Here you can see a group of hungry raccoons in a Washington backyard. They were drawn to the smell of dog food, which they dumped on the ground and started to eat.

Raccoons are **omnivores**, which means that they eat both plants and animals. The list of things raccoons eat is very long! It includes acorns and other nuts, berries, fruit, garden crops, crayfish, frogs, clams, fish, turtles, worms, and turtle and bird eggs—even people's garbage! Sometimes raccoons also eat **carrion**, which is the meat of dead animals.

Raccoons are known as "opportunistic feeders," which means they will eat almost anything, as long as it's easy to get.

Raccoons raid insect nests, including hornets' or bees' nests, to eat the wormlike insect larvae. The raccoons' thick fur helps protect them from the adult insects' stings.

This adult raccoon is eating the fish it just caught. You can see how the raccoon holds its meal with its sharp claws.

17

How Do Raccoons Eat Their Food?

Raccoons can use their slender fingers to untie knots, turn doorknobs, open catches, and even open jars.

Scientists name animals in the ancient language of Latin. The scientific name for raccoons is *Procyon lotor* (PRO-see-un LOW-tor). "Lotor" means "one who washes."

Raccoons use their front paws to reach and climb and to grab the things they eat. In fact, they usually use their front paws to pick up their food before they eat it. A raccoon's front paws are almost as useful as your hands. The raccoon can use them to crack open crayfish shells or even unlock food coolers!

Before raccoons eat, they sometimes dip their food in water. Many people believe they do this to clean their food, but that isn't true. Raccoons' front paws are very sensitive. Scientists think water helps the raccoons feel for food and also feel for parts of the food they should throw away.

Here you can see a raccoon dipping its food in a Pennsylvania stream. It dunked and rubbed the food several times before taking a bite.

What Are Baby Raccoons Like?

Raccoon kits are only about 6 inches (15 cm) long when they are born.

A mother raccoon carries her babies the way a mother cat does—by the scruff of the neck.

Raccoon kits sound a lot like whining puppies.

During January or February, a male and a female raccoon mate. After mating, the two raccoons go back to their own dens. Nine weeks later, the female gives birth to about five baby raccoons. The babies, called **kits**, are very tiny. They have no teeth yet, and their eyelids won't open. In two to three weeks, their eyes open, their teeth start to grow in, and the kits begin to move around.

About two months after they are born, the babies start following their mother out of the den. The mother teaches them how to climb, swim, and search for food. When they are several months old, the young raccoons go off to live on their own.

These raccoon kits are peeking out of their den on a sunny spring day.

20

Do Raccoons Have Enemies?

Raccoons would rather escape than fight, but when cornered, they are tough fighters. An adult raccoon can kill a dog.

Raccoons can run at speeds up to 15 miles (24 km) per hour. They are also strong swimmers.

Adult raccoons don't have many natural enemies, but foxes, owls, and bobcats all eat young raccoons if given the chance. When a raccoon is fully grown, few animals want to face its sharp teeth and claws.

Most wild raccoons don't live past their second year. If they aren't killed by other animals, raccoons often die from accidents, disease, or lack of food. If they do make it through their first two years, raccoons often live to be about seven. In rare cases, wild raccoons can live up to 16 years.

22

Here you can see a coyote chasing an adult raccoon in Montana. Coyotes don't hunt raccoons very often, because raccoons can put up such a tough fight. Old or sick raccoons have less chance of fighting off an attacker.

The main enemies of healthy adult raccoons are people. Many raccoons are hit by cars or trucks as they cross roads or feed on dead animals along the roadside. Some people trap raccoons for their fur or hunt them for food or sport.

Raccoons are also killed by people who find them to be pests. Sometimes people get tired of raccoons living around their homes or buildings or raiding their garbage. Farmers and gardeners sometimes kill raccoons to stop them from eating their crops.

People sometimes use raccoon skins to make clothing. Coonskin caps have the raccoon's tail still hanging down in back. Big coats made of coonskin were popular in the 1920s.

No one is sure how many raccoons are killed by cars and trucks every year, but it might be as many as several million.

This adult raccoon was out searching for food—in the middle of the day! Raccoons sometimes hunt for their meals during the daytime, but only if they are very hungry.

25

Are Raccoons Dangerous?

Pet dogs and cats get shots of a vaccine that keeps them from getting rabies.

In rare cases, very young children have ended up with raccoon roundworm from playing where raccoons had lived. They probably got dirt on their hands and then put their hands in their mouths.

The greatest danger from raccoons is that they often carry diseases, including a serious disease called **rabies**. In North America, the four wild animals most likely to carry rabies are raccoons, skunks, foxes, and bats. Without the right kind of treatment, the bite of an animal with rabies leads to death. Because of the danger of disease, people should never go near wild raccoons. Anyone who is bitten should wash the bite carefully and get to a doctor right away.

Another problem is a kind of roundworm that lives in raccoons' bodies. The raccoons pass the roundworm eggs in their body waste. Even after the waste breaks down, the eggs can last in the soil for years. Animals or people who accidentally eat the eggs can get very sick and die.

Here a scientist is putting an ear tag on a raccoon. Tagging raccoons doesn't harm them, and it helps scientists study raccoon diseases. This raccoon was caught in a cage and given some medicine to make it sleep. The scientist took some blood to check for rabies and other diseases. After getting its tag, the raccoon will be returned to the forest, where it will wake up and be on its way.